S0-ESD-454

How To Wait

poems by

Erin M. Kelly

Finishing Line Press
Georgetown, Kentucky

How To Wait

Copyright © 2018 by Erin M. Kelly
ISBN 978-1-63534-485-1 First Edition
All rights reserved under International and Pan-American Copyright Conventions. No part of this book may be reproduced in any manner whatsoever without written permission from the publisher, except in the case of brief quotations embodied in critical articles and reviews.

ACKNOWLEDGMENTS

Special thanks to the following publications for publishing works in this collection during various stages of their development:

-*Wordgathering, A Journal of Disability Poetry and Literature*
-*Oberon Poetry Magazine*

Publisher: Leah Maines
Editor: Christen Kincaid
Cover Art: Christie Clancy, www.clancy214photography.com
Author Photo: Christie Clancy, www.clancy214photography.com
Cover Design: Elizabeth Maines McCleavy

Printed in the USA on acid-free paper.
Order online: www.finishinglinepress.com
also available on amazon.com

Author inquiries and mail orders:
Finishing Line Press
P. O. Box 1626
Georgetown, Kentucky 40324
U. S. A.

Table of Contents

Introduction
How to Wait 1
I Can't Win or Lose 3
Parade 4
Autograph 5
Foresight 6
Celebrity under My Skin 7
Junior High 8
Aging Views 9
Permanence: The Season's Stain 10
The Controller 11
Horoscope 12
Today 13
A Long Way from Hello 14
When the World Breaks 15
Acceptance (Your Turn) 16
Matchbox 17
Fight from the Outside 18
Turning Point 19
The Journalist's Prayer 20
The Poet and the Apprentice 21
Daybreak 22
Saturday Moments 23
Dream Catcher 24
Happy Girl Syndrome 25
All Eyes on Life 26
Sunshine 27
The Journey 28
Teacher 29
The Walk 30
Tainted Remedy 31

*For everyone who has believed in me,
and who's taught me that it truly takes a village to raise a child.*

Introduction

Poetry is an art form—perhaps the most unrestricting, freeing platforms of all genres in the literary world. For me, it stands at the core of why I immersed myself into the creative, yet relentlessly difficult work of being a writer, journalist, and poet. When I first started out, I was told by many of my college professors—who were already at the top of their writing game with multiple books published—that I had "magic" in my fingers, and that I should attempt to pursue a career as a writer or poet.

I'd never heard either part of that compliment before. I was always encouraged by my family when I was a little girl. They always knew I wanted to be something bigger than myself, but hearing this from people who were outside my immediate circle was huge. It opened my eyes to the possibilities that come from creativity, but more importantly, it would end up becoming the beginning of a journey that fit my life like a glove.

As a woman with cerebral palsy, I see the world through different eyes than those around me. My life is often like a video game as I navigate through my immediate surroundings. By the same token, those surroundings are sometimes all I have to build the foundation of a poem off of—and because my circumstances make it difficult for me to be understood, I don't always have the opportunity to express myself with spoken words—the way I'd like to be heard.

The original poems in this book are a culmination and reflection of that. Each one is an open letter to the world, wrapped in the layers of language—the language I'm most comfortable with as a woman. They're a snapshot of what I see, think, and feel, and mirror what happened the very moment I fell in love with the power of words. Most importantly, they reflect all the things people haven't heard from me directly.

Some of these poems are sad, some happy, and some come from deep, dark places, as good poetry often does. However, all of them were written with a human heart. My human heart. As you read on, know that I do have a voice. You just have to listen.

How to Wait
> *"Patience and fortitude conquer all things."*
> ~Ralph Waldo Emerson

Watch the illuminated stripes
on your wall
brighten and fade through
thin rows of window blinds.

They'll crawl to the floor soon,
like dancers with ladybugs
in their pants.

Listen for the door of your entrance and exit
to leave a trail of windburn.

In a minute,
tempered voices will
slam it shut again.

Sometimes you wish
you could inject
a dose of velvety chocolate
into their throats.

Feel the hand of aid
from your junior high past
sweep the bed sheets
off your warm body.

She's waiting to smother you with lotion…

…to lift and touch you
like a burning spirit.

When you're up,
go to your computer
and read messages
you never want to erase.

Pray and thank your god
for everything
you've still got.

It's only 9:30 a.m.

I Can't Win or Lose

I'm spinning in circles,
clutching the control of my life.

All names can see my story, but not
all lips ask my name.

All bodies look like mine when
they sit in a chair…

…except when lives walk away from
pieces of existence
spilt on poker tables.

Parade

Diseases in suits walk the streets,
where I write for
the company of empty minds.

I watch blimps float passed
fields of comprehension.

I look down.

Children try to laugh while
building sandcastles on concrete.

They throw down their tools
when they see a waste of age
behind a clown's face paint…

…but wait, here come pretty little lies
dressed in a woman's lipstick.

I heard she always uses
the glow from a cigarette to
find her way home.

I look up.

Blackened hands chisel bricks
off of weathered buildings, but can't
lift the haze off my front lawn.

Criminals congregate on the fence,
hung over a drunken moon.

Has everyone kissed the enemy?

No, I guess it's just me now.

Autograph
    For Erin Murphy

I was a sophomore when
I bought her first book.

Its title reminded me of the
many times I tried to
pull science out of the stars.

A stream of fresh ink
ran through her name.

It was my name too,
only with five more letters
before the Y.

Some may mistake it for a
slip of the hand or
a rush of blood to the head…

…but it's just a treasure from a conscious world.

Foresight
> *For Patricia Jabbeh-Wesley*

When I first heard your words,
you were my teacher.

I knew there was a world of poetry
inside you, but didn't know
there was one inside me.

You said poetry could take
a soul to the moon, or be as
as close to the heart as kin...

... but I still needed to see that for myself.

When it was time for the student to
become the teacher, you signed my book and
set me on a path to the stars.

All before you knew what I'd become,
and said those words
before I had a bottle to keep them in.

I haven't reached the top of the mountain
you're sitting upon, but I'm on my way.

Celebrity under My Skin

I pen my identity into the
fabric of your conscience, watching
as you tilt the sun towards me.

You say I've got "it" and
ask if I take the orange stripe
out of a rainbow to burn
my dreams into a skyline.

Every page you read has been
stained and painted
like a wooden soldier…

…I just never expected these thoughts
would ever come out of my basement.

Junior High

Back in those halls,
a skateboarder got
twisted on a high rail…

…baseball player hit the bases too hard.

Laughter tasted like
a lollipop that lingered.

Immaturity lit fires,
smelling like the twang
in a country song.

Lessons sold respect like
front page news,
but knowledge
didn't read its palm.

I'm sure life wasn't
aware that science
could see it all.

Aging Views

From here, it sounds like
birds sing with a
broken piece of glass
piercing their throats.

The effects fall on you.

You shove another
candle into that 23rd cake,
and light it
like a dream.

It's yours, but
nothing's been passed on.

You tell yourself that
the next twelve months will
add up to a good reason
to waste away.

It feels like eleven months have
already went by.

As you try to lick the
sweet sap from winter trees,
I ask myself:

Will I swallow fame
before smoke rings
have a chance to breathe?

Permanence: The Season's Stain

When the sun rises,
I take the fortress of faces
I've built with my time, and
test its strength underneath

the heat of the season.

I'd wait to pick up the falling pieces,
but there are none.

In truth, selfish reasons could
burn, blister my beliefs in the newness
these faces bring, but
I've got their personalities stamped on
the back of my hand—and don't let the ink run.

Mother even says my strength lies between
the clock's twelve numbers and two hands,
while I remind myself my faith is enough.

The Controller

You offer me a seat
stuffed with seconds
and minutes.

You cause riots
I've learned to hush,
even though you don't
have a rear-view mirror
to see what you've done.

Here's the road where
my fingers gush poetic blood,
the one Frost said was
less traveled upon.

We're passing the places
where some hearts have
no place to change.

Sometimes I get too
far ahead, asking my brothers
to take this ride.

I wish we could tell them
how far we've gone,
but miles were always our
best-kept secret.

Horoscope

In ten years,
my story will be a
full body with a
pierced belly button.

I'll be reminded of the heaviness
absence carries every time
I slip my finger through
that titanium loop.

Goodbyes will credit themselves
as angels whose wings
needed to be clipped.

When names are finally recycled,
everyone will have
a piece of me.

Today

I remember when decades
claimed you as a boy.

You kept track of miles
in your footsteps and dropped
letters at the gates of Heaven.

You saved the gray
for a rainy day, the deepest
blue for the darkest night.

Now, as a father,
you take the orange from
all these sunsets and
write home about
how to feed a child.

So tell me where to start.

Tell me where to start to
paint pictures of life that
make me feel real.

A Long Way from Hello

April was the first time
I threw my body
into the sea of distance.

I threw my watch in first,
but its face floated to the surface
and the hands rose above.

I'd show you where the bridge breaks,
but friends are still walking across it.

They're headed for train stops and airports.

Then they wait in first class
to arrive in places
my wheels don't dare spin.

With one quick flip of the wrist,
we find ourselves conversing through
wires and letters that we hope will
never tear or tangle.

When the World Breaks

The sky will be
pregnant with dreams.

Children will throw down
questions of soldiers and devils,
wondering which one will
dawn the red and blue suit first—
if at all.

We'll sit and watch
kings and queens
breathe heavy, hot air
in this game of chess.

Acceptance (Your Turn)

If you can shape my dictionary to
fit everything that bears your name,
I'll find you somewhere
in me, lost.

If you can't find a way out,
turn the music up.

Your ears will shiver in the
world's nakedness, but
inside those headphones…

…inside the words
you've heard
and are too afraid to
dance to…

…truth doesn't play games.

Matchbox

I've wanted to light a match so many times,
but grace comes like a thief in the night.

I lie in bed, take the matchbox out from
underneath pillow, and let its warmth singe my hand.

Too many matches have been lit
by silly default.

They've been lit on a word, a promise of
 good company that never seems to make it
over the threshold.

I have too many friends living in different zip codes.

I'm not even sure if their town has a zip code.

Can I blame distance?

Can I blame the disgusting
appeal of a promise?

Selfishness?

My matchbox is still hot from my hand.

I wonder if I can fit my doubt in there,
instead of these old matches?

Fight from the Outside

Will they find a cure?

I ask that to
whatever's left…

…or whoever listens.

There's still so much left to do, but
I've got a thin coat over me now.

I don't want to admit I've
never been seen naked.

You tried to choke this
plague with both hands before—
and when you escaped it yourself,
your sixth sister rejoiced.

She'd still call you beautiful,
even though
I am left cold.

Turning Point

I see lives move so fast,
they've got time
wrapped around their finger.

Hands are the ultimate
manipulators, pulling you
underneath the wheel.

Now you're breathless
because you forgot to
leave a light on.

I'm different.

I take my time when
I've got a thousand beats
in my system.

They dance slowly like
a pancake breakfast should
on a Sunday morning.

My hands follow along,
words flowing from the
fingertips the way time trickles
out of a calendar day.

If I could set the pace of the world,
you would never come and go again.

The Journalist's Prayer

Today, I wake up and
measure accuracy by the words
written in black and white.

Common folk with two working legs
carry stories home
on their backs as I try to trace
the lines on their faces.

I wonder what I'm doing
writing about a man
who scribbles his sins
on an index card…

…when I really want to know why
the sky never seems to be the right shade
of blue for those who can afford to
walk beside their own shadow.

They've got two legs, two feet that
feel at home on concrete and carpet.

I've got two hands that
feel at home on a keyboard.

Maybe tomorrow, they'll wake up and
see they've got more than me—instead of
falling asleep with their hands shoved in
a pocketful of complaints.

The Poet and the Apprentice
For Cameron Conaway

They call you The Warrior Poet, but before 2012,
I didn't know who you were—or that poets
could even be warriors.

I didn't know how one goes about
earning that name or wearing the
clothes that go with it.

I just had magic in my fingers—and
when I told you about the silent war I'd
been fighting, you already knew of my scars.

You invited me into your world, to put
that pain against a white canvas and
let it breathe in the light of day, and
thrive in the darkness of night.

You knew pain too, so you taught me
how to bleed through words.

You did it without reading my "disabled"
label or judging me by the seat I sit in.

Now the stories I write aren't just mine.

So, what do you say when a stranger
becomes a teacher, when a poet gives
you more than just his pen?

I don't know, but I hope to one day be
wearing your warrior clothes.

Daybreak

Love is the teacher who
puts on his shoes while the city sleeps to
try to pave the way for change.

He doesn't know if his words
will stick in between the pages of history—
or be on the tongues of those he's taught.

He's traveled the world, writing years' worth
of poems and anecdotes that have likely been
recited by scientists and strangers…

…but he knows his pride will always be
on the mantle at home—

where his wife stays by his side,
with a ring and a promise.

When dusk falls, he'll know she's
his bones, his blood, his bride.

And her faithful heart never dies.

Saturday Moments

I am a song,
rising in a robe…

…or sometimes in boxer shorts.

That first mouthful of coffee
trickles down my bones.

Sometimes I hear
the bare bones
of notes I missed.

Melodies repeated.

I listen and play along until
I get the right tone…

..the strings vibrate,
and I wonder how
I could ever leave this moment
alone.

The lights flicker.

Cords sink in.

I've raised three voices
and together,
They are my song.

Dream Catcher

> *"Set a goal, clear a path, and go after what you want."*
> ~Dwayne "The Rock" Johnson

Hunger is a paid resident of
a one-room house.

It stays overnight and
soaks into your bed sheets
like a secret.

At night, sleep on your beautiful stains—
because in the morning,
you'll make a fresh batch of mistakes.

Desire will try to run away.

Snatch it…

…be willing to bleed.

Happy Girl Syndrome

The posters on my wall depict
bodies of work that
tussle in spandex underwear.

I keep my ten-year old confessions
in my front pocket
as I watch sweat
roll off washboard stomachs
like tears of victory.

The arm of the victor
is raised, showing his
leopard skin tattoos.

They glisten through
a coat of baby oil,
as thick as muscles
running on adrenaline.

My pupils are still
popping out like
3-D sunspots, but
you can call this
an obsession.

All Eyes on Life

Almost two decades
claim you as a boy,
but your actions
fit in a man's shoe size.

Days pass in the
palm of your hand.

At sunset,
you lay them down
in your dreams, and
step harder the next day
so memories can stay in
footsteps left behind.

Prayer writes your wishes
to Heaven in midnight hours.

If only gun powder, wounds, and bombs
held a smile, life would disarm
everything you could've been.

I don't know how you weren't
bruised when the war
decided to go East, but
your arms were always
wider than mine.

Sunshine

Love starts as a seed that's
planted in the soul.

It grows in the brightest of lights,
and blooms in the highest of hopes.

It walks the roughest roads,
and always finds its way.

Love is the smile on your face that
never seems to fade away.

The Journey

It started with one.

One sunrise.
One crossroad.
One culture.

But the wind blew until
there were two of everything…

…until a girl grew into a woman,
and a man gave her his word.

Colors began to blend and
families celebrated the union.

Now there's an altar up ahead,
forever merging the lives they've led.

Teacher

I came to you
with a dream.

I gave it a heartbeat,
but it needed a face.

You taught me to
dig into my own soul.

You're a dream keeper who
told me to read the stars
like a second language.

The Walk

I heard you've been traveling
a rough road.

I heard you've been smiling while
your heart mends.

Somewhere along the way, you
taught me how to be a friend.

You taught me to slow down and smile.

Your footsteps never got too far ahead
or behind, always staying with me.

In any weather, you were there.

Now, as you go down this long road, know that
I'll always do the same for you.

Tainted Remedy

A room full of whispers
is a court of beggars with the
salt from tears
lodged in their voices.

Buds of sunshine
sit on tables
cut to fit corners
everyone has to turn.

The life in the box
In front of me
says to keep going…

…keep writing the words
I write and praise smiles at
the sound of.

My own tears bleed
on the product of a tree
and clot on the
brittle promise of willpower…

…but as I sit here looking on,
you're still smiling at those
words inside the crash.

E**rin M. Kelly's** path to becoming a writer began with a simple box of crayons she had as a child. Her mind went on autopilot as her hand drew brilliant streaks of blue, red, and every other color of a rainbow. She utilized her creativity as a way to not only learn to live with her diagnosis of cerebral palsy, but to understand it. Most of all, she wanted to be seen, heard, and understood. Erin's willingness to learn about the craft of writing and editing has led to her chosen career.

She is a now writer, journalist, columnist, freelance editor and poet who enjoys writing in all genres. She wants to be recognized for her work rather than her disability. Her work has been published by *The Huffington Post, Upworthy, The Mighty, The Good Men Project, Wordgathering Poetry Journal, XoJane,* and *Oberon Poetry Magazine.*

Erin also writes a monthly column entitled, "The View from Here," for the local newspaper in Altoona, Pennsylvania, addressing the challenges she faces daily. She served as Editor for the memoir, To Cope and To Prevail, by Dr. Ilse-Rose Warg. Writing is her window to the world giving her the opportunity to bring what's inside out.

Through her twenty-year journey, Erin has learned the importance of responsibility and kindness. Her writing has provided a platform for her to educate and entertain readers with a mindful purpose: to let others know that disability in general is not something to be feared, but rather, embraced. More importantly, Erin writes to spread her message that she wants to be treated the same as everyone she meets. She does it all knowing that writing, and the uniquely hectic life that comes with it, is a conscious choice. She's forever grateful for everyone who chose to come along for the ride!